Katrin Unterreiner

Sissi

Empress Elisabeth of Austria

With photos by Willfried Gredler-Oxenbauer

D1734895

pichler verlag

EMPRESS ELISABETH
"OUT IN THE WORLD TITANIA SHALL NOT GO"

On 24 April 1854, when at the tender age of 16 the Bavarian Princess Elisabeth married her cousin, Austrian Emperor Franz Joseph I, the newlyweds were considered a dream couple. Yet the reality of it was much different. From the first day on, Elisabeth felt alone, patronised and uncomfortable in her role as Empress of Austria. Initially she tried to fulfil what was expected of her, but her duties as empress made her feel uncomfortable; representation as well as the strict court etiquette she found increasingly burdensome. She detested the rigid hierarchical structures of the Viennese court and also found no fulfilment in her role as mother. Yet over time Sissi, as Elisabeth was called by her family, learned to assert herself against the Viennese court. The empress recognised the power of her beauty, used it for her personal interests and, outside of the Viennese court, lived a life that corresponded with her own ideas. The empress became one of the best parforce riders of her time, went on extended trips, and spent most of her time abroad. But although she was able to arrange her life freely and was anything but caught in a golden cage, she was not happy. She may have refused to fulfil the traditional duties of empress, wife and mother that were expected of her by the court and society, but she didn't look for any other fulfilling task. In her later years the empress withdrew more and more from the public eye, became unsociable and unapproachable. She wrote melancholy poems, identified with the fairy queen Titania from Shakespeare's *Midsummer Night's Dream* and wrote: "Out in the world Titania shall not go / A world where she is never understood".

Following the suicide of her son, Crown Prince Rudolf, Elisabeth only wore black, and most people only experienced her as a black silhouette in the distance. Depression and thoughts of death increasingly enveloped her. On 10 September 1898, when Elisabeth was murdered by the Italian anarchist Luigi Lucheni in Geneva, her daughter Marie Valerie wrote in her journal: "Now it has happened just as she always wished: quickly, painlessly without medical consultations; without long, anxious days of worry for her loved ones.". When Emperor Franz Joseph, who loved his wife unconditionally her whole life long, heard of the death of his "Sissi angel" his only words were: "You have no idea what this woman meant to me".

Left page: Posthumous portrait of Empress Elisabeth by Gyula Benczur, around 1898.
Above: In front of Emperor Franz Joseph's desk in the Vienna Hofburg was his favourite portrait of Elisabeth by Franz Xaver Winterhalter, showing the empress with her hair open.

"I AM A CHILD OF THE SUN"

The signs were significant and promising: Elisabeth Amalie Eugenia, the third child of Duke Max in Bavaria and the Bavarian Princess Ludovika, was born on 24 December 1837, on Christmas Eve, which also happened to be a Sunday, with a tooth, which was regarded as a particularly lucky sign. Because Elisabeth's father belonged to a branch of the Wittelsbachs, he didn't have an official function at the Munich court and the family didn't have any ceremonial duties. So Sissi – as Elisabeth was called in family circles – was able to grow up free and unconstrained in Palais Max on Ludwigstrasse in Munich. The summer was spent at the family at Schloss Possenhofen on Lake Starnberg, removed from etiquette, ceremony and the constraints of the court. Sissi loved the summer months in "Possi", as Possenhofen was called by the family, where she and her siblings Ludwig, Helene ("Néné"), Carl Theodor ("Gackel"), Marie, Mathilde ("Spatz"), Sophie and Max Emmanuel ("Mapperl") were able to spend most of their time outdoors. Sissi took after her father in many ways. The duke had an unconventional lifestyle, loved nature, was a passionate rider and took extended trips. From him, the children learned to love nature and the joys of physical exercise, which, mainly for girls back at the time, was absolutely unusual. While other girls of her age and standing were embroidering and sewing and learning foreign languages, dancing, music and conversation, Sissi and her siblings spent the whole summer running around outside, hiking, horseback riding and swimming. Elisabeth later told her Greek reader Constantin Christomanos, who was amazed by the empress' stamina on their mutual walks, "I also never get tired … We, my sisters and I, have our father to thank for this. 'One also must learn to walk well', he always told us, and engaged a private tutor to teach us."

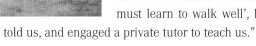

Left page: Portrait of the young Elisabeth by the Munich photographer Franz Hanfstaengl.
Above: Sissi, aged 11, with her favourite brother, Carl Theodor, nicknamed "Gackl", 1849.

Duke Max in Bavaria influenced his children with his unconventional way of life. He was politically liberal, educated and realised his personal life style. As Elisabeth later did, he also fled protocol and idyllic family life, didn't want to subject himself to constraints; was interested in many different things, adventurous – and travelled a lot. According to this, Elisabeth didn't develop into a rebellious outsider, but stayed loyal to the family tradition her whole life.

Her parents' marriage was not a happy one; the interests and temperament of the two were too different. Ludovika devotedly looked after the children; Duke Max, on the other hand, didn't think much of a homely family life and spent most of his time with his hobbies – travelling, circus and drinking sessions in his bourgeois circle of friends – as well as with his lovers and numerous extra-marital children.

Above: Elisabeth on the banks of the Starnberg Lake, lithography by Eduard Kaiser, 1853/54.
Left page, below: View of Possenhofen Castle at Lake Starnberg, gouache, 1854

"O, MY LORD, WHAT A BEAUTEOUS DREAM"
Engagement in Ischl

In summer 1853 an encounter took place in Bad Ischl, Salkammergut, that would go down in the history books. As he did every year, Emperor Franz Joseph celebrated his birthday in the spa town, to which the Habsburgs had a particular relationship. His mother, Archduchess Sophie, had been there several times as a young woman for the salt water spa treatments, her sojourns were followed by the yearned for pregnancies, which is why Franz Joseph and his brother were also called the 'Salt Princes'". On the emperor's twenty-third birthday, on 18 August, his aunt Ludovika in Bavaria was invited there with her daughters Helene, known as Néné, and Elisabeth. The actual reason for this trip were wedding plans, which the mothers of the couple were hatching. Franz Joseph, who was looking for a wife, was supposed to get to know his cousins, whom he hadn't seen since he was a child, and was then supposed to choose one of the two princesses to be his wife. At first sight, Franz Joseph really fell in love with the 15-year-old Sissi. His mother described the decisive moment in a letter. "... The

moment the emperor laid his eyes on Sissi an expression of such satisfaction came across his face that there was no more doubt which one he was going to choose. He was beaming, and you know how his face beams when he is happy. The lovely Sissi had no idea of the lasting impression that she had made on Franzi. Up to this moment, because her mother had mentioned it to her, she became bashful and shy among the many people in her environment [...] And she was so pretty and charming doing so!" As early as 19 August, the celebratory engagement took place, and Sissi became shy and quiet at the huge amount of attention she was receiving; Franz Joseph on the other hand, was overjoyed. Incidentally, his mother Archduchess Sophie was not, as is often suggested, against the choice of her son. On the contrary, as part of the first public appearance at Franz Joseph's birthday ball, she raved about Sissi and described her as "so charming, so modest, so immaculate, graceful ..." and was above all happy to see her son so happy.

Left page: Anonymous portrait of the imperial bride aged 16.
Above: Transfiguring idyll: Duke Max in Bavaria, Emperor Franz Joseph and Sissi during a boat trip on Lake Starnberg. Lithography, 1853.

Emperor Franz Joseph and Elisabeth. Lithographies by R. Hoffmann after Anton Einsle, 1854.

First excursion of the newlyweds in Ischl. Painting by Johann Gottlieb Prestel, ca. 1853/54.

On the evening before Sissi's departure to Vienna for her wedding a farewell ball was held in Munich at which Sissi wore a particularly eccentric dress. The Ottoman embroidery on the dress and the accompanying stole tellingly says, "Oh, my Lord, what a beauteous dream".

BAD ISCHL
The "earthly heaven" – Imperial family summer

When Emperor Franz saw his cousin Elisabeth again he was immediately taken by her grace and her girl-like charm and gushed, "No, how sweet Sissi is. She's fresh like a jumping jack and what a magnificent crown of hair frames her face! Such lovely, soft eyes and lips like strawberries!" Just one day later he exuberantly announced his engagement. Shortly thereafter, Franz Joseph's mother Archduchess Sophie bought Villa Eltz in Ischl and, in 1854, complete with the associated grounds, gave it to newly-wed imperial couple at their wedding. The villa was remodelled to what today is the Kaiservilla and became a summer refuge for the imperial family, to which the emperor could flee with his family "from the paper-dominated, desk-bound existence with its anxieties and troubles."

In memory of the happy time of their engagement Ischl became the private favourite residency of the imperial couple, a place they particularly enjoyed the few days they were able to spend together undisturbed as a family in nature, and also where they celebrated every birthday of the emperor. In Ischl the imperial family, away from courtly etiquette and representative duties, felt particularly comfortable. This is where they were able to enjoy a harmonious family life, and above all Franz Joseph, who described Ischl as his "earthly heaven", loved the weeks with his daughters and grandchildren, with whom he spent a great deal of time.

Upon Empress Elisabeth's insistence, Emperor Franz Joseph, as early as 1887, decreed that their youngest, favourite daughter, Archduchess Marie Valerie, should later inherit the Kaiservilla, including its grounds. Even after the end of the monarchy, in the year 1918, the Kaiservilla remained in the possession of the family Habsburg-Lorraine, because Marie Valerie had relinquished her and her descendants' rights to the throne and for this reason, due to her maintaining her private assets, was able to stay in Austria.

Right page, below: Family dinner in Ischl with Emperor Franz Joseph, Empress Elisabeth, their daughter Marie Valerie, her husband, Archduke Franz Salvator, their daughter Gisela and her husband, Georg of Bavaria, as well as their sons Leopold and Konrad.
Drawing by Theo Zasche around 1890.

Below: Emperor Franz Joseph with his grandchildren in the Kaiservilla park around 1910.

Above: In Ischl in the year 1854, Duchess Sophie purchased the property of the Viennese notary August Elz for the newlywed Imperial couple. The renovations to the imperial summer villa weren't finished until 1865. Both side wings were added; afterwards, Elisabeth lived in the centre tract. In the new western tract (left) were Franz Joseph's apartments and in the eastern tract (right), the room for the children.

"YOU WILL BE FOR HIM AN ISLAND, WHICH AMIDST THE CRASHING WAVES WILL BE A HAVEN"
Wedding in Vienna

On 20 April 1854, Elisabeth left Munich, accompanied by her parents and both her older siblings Ludwig and Néné. From Straubing they sailed on ships decorated with flowers towards Vienna, where on 22 April the imperial bride was received by Franz Joseph, the entire imperial family and the dignitaries of the empire ceremoniously. The next day there was a celebratory procession in the city and in the Hofburg. But Elisabeth was overwhelmed by the many impressions, the expectations and the thousand spectators, so the Viennese didn't see a glowing bride but an exhausted, frightened and crying girl.

On the evening of the 24 April 1854, the wedding finally took place in the Viennese Augustinerkirche, the parish church of the Hofburg. The church was festively decorated – up to the ceiling with gold-embroidered damask and lit with thousands of candles. The monarchy presented itself from its most luxurious side. Following the ceremony the wedding party went to the Hofburg, where the ministers, diplomats and envoys had collected in the secret council chambers. On this, her wedding day, Elisabeth is supposed to have been introduced to her future life as empress – for there was no cheerful ball, but the newly married couple first received all dignitaries of the country; afterwards the empress was officially introduced to the royal household. Among them were also the newly chosen palace and apartment ladies, who in future would be the only ones allowed to enter the empress' apartment, and were exclusively chosen based on their rank and standing.

Elisabeth felt uncomfortable with all the attention that was being showered on her as bride – but was mainly overwhelmed by the exhausting programme. During the first reception as the new empress she broke into tears from exhaustion and left the hall.

In the days following her wedding there were other public appointments and ceremonies that she had to attend – receptions of various country delegations, court dinners and balls. One exception was the peoples' festival in the Prater on Saturday 29 April, at which the famous Circus Renz also performed their riding skills. It was the only celebration that made Elisabeth happy.

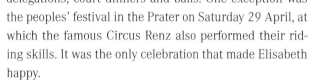

Left page: The wedding of Emperor Franz Joseph and Elisabeth Duchess in Bavaria took place on 24 April in the Augustinerkirche in Vienna. Wood engraving from *Neue Illustrierte Zeitung*, 1879.
Above: Wedding announcement of the Imperial couple.

The young Imperial couple. Contemporary depiction.

The dowry of the young bride. Elisabeth's dowry consisted of jewellery, gold vessels, gems, silver and her wardrobe. For an empress-to-be, it was extremely modest.

First reception of the newlywed Imperial couple in the Hofburg. Contemporary wood engraving.

The young Imperial couple on a walk on Gloriettehügel in Schönbrunn. Contemporary lithography.

Below: On the occasion of the Imperial couple's wedding a large public celebration was held at which the newlyweds were presented to the Viennese public in the festively decorated Prater. Anonymous lithography.

HOFBURG
The imperial apartments in the Vienna Hofburg

From the beginning of the Habsburg rule in Austria in the 13th century until the end of the monarchy in the year 1918, the Vienna Hofburg was the main residence of the imperial family. But it was more than that – with 18 tracts and over 2,600 rooms, it was a city within a city in which up to 2,000 people lived and worked. Every Habsburg ruler left behind his or her traces and influenced the look of the Hofburg with their respective lifestyles.

In the year 1857 Emperor Franz Joseph and Empress Elisabeth moved into the apartments of the Reichskanzleitrakt and had the rooms remodelled according to what was in style at the time, Neo Rococo. The rosewood and nutwood walls and furniture were covered with red silk damask, the pattern of which showed ear of corn as a symbol of fertility. The rooms were heated with ceramic tiled stoves, though only accessible from outside – from a passage behind the walls – in order not to bother the imperial family and not to dirty the rooms. The chandeliers made from Bohemian lead crystal were originally lit with candles. It wasn't until the year 1891 that electricity was installed in the Hofburg. The Imperial Apartments, which in recent years have been restored and refurbished in historically authentic style, not only give an impression of imperial living culture but also an idea of the imperial family's day-to-day life, showing glimpses of the monarchs as well as the private and family people.

Left: Franz Joseph and Elisabeth at the breakfast table. Drawing by Theo Zasche, around 1890.

Below: Begun in 1575, finished in 1611 by Pietro Ferabosco, the Amalienburg was named after Joseph I's widow, Empress Amalie, who resided here until 1742. In the second half of the 19th century, on the first floor along the Burgplatz, were Empress Elisabeth's living quarters, which after her death in 1898 until the end of the monarchy remained unchanged and can be viewed today.

Opposite page: At the end of the 19th century the Michaelertrakt gave the Hofburg a representative facade facing the inner city, and with its 54-metre-high dome was a landmark visible for miles away. The cast iron gate represented the new official entrance to the Hofburg from the inner-city side and led to the Michaelerkuppel, where the Imperial couple disembarked from their carriage and accessed their apartments.

Above: The empress spent most of her time in her dressing room and exercise room. For two hours a day her hair was dressed while she learned languages or had someone read to her. It caused a great stir that she exercised here daily in order to keep fit for her riding, which she engaged in as a high-performance sport. Today the exercise equipment she used – wall bars, horizontal bar and rings that were mounted on the door frame – are still preserved. After exercising, the empress was massaged on the small divan.

Left: In 1876, Empress Elisabeth was the first member of the imperial house to have her own bathroom installed. Her bath tub made of galvanised sheet copper is still preserved today, albeit without the original ceramic insert and the fixtures. At the same time, the first toilet in the Hofburg was installed for the empress – in the form of a dolphin. Until then, only room toilets had been used in the court, which had to be carried into the room when needed; bathrooms and toilets were seen as superfluous luxuries.

Right, above: The empress' living room and bedroom. Elisabeth used the room that was directly connected to the emperor's apartment as well as the bedroom and the salon, in which, during the day, the bed was simply removed from the room.

Right, below: Family dinners were held in the early evening for the family members and guests of honour were staying in Vienna. Even the family meals followed a strict ceremony – one was only allowed to speak to one's immediate neighbour and never converse with anyone across the table. The meals were brought from the court kitchen to the apartments in warmed boxes and prepared in a side room. A dinner usually consisted of 9 to 12 courses and usually took about an hour.

"IF ONLY I HAD ALWAYS STAYED/ ON FREEDOM'S PATHWAY BLESSED"
The young empress

Elisabeth's expectations of her marriage were quickly dashed. She would get an impression of her future daily life as early as during her honeymoon, for even as a newlywed, Franz Joseph saw himself as firstly an emperor, who had to fulfil his obligations, and spent the whole day working. Sissi was disappointed, felt lonely and isolated, yet never alone, for her every move was monitored and observed. Mainly by her mother-in-law Archduchess Sophie – who didn't involve herself in her niece's life out of maliciousness, but because she saw it as her duty to make a perfect empress out of the shy 16-year-old girl. Despite all preparation, however, Sissi had a difficult time coming to terms with her new life situation. She felt patronised, and her difficulties adjusting raised hackles with the ceremonious Viennese court. At first she tried to fulfil the expectations placed on her, however her duties as empress made her feel uncomfortable; representation as well as the strict court etiquette she found increasingly burdensome and she detested the rigid hierarchical structures of the Viennese court. Franz Joseph loved Elisabeth above all else, but he left her alone with her fears and distress. As early as 8 May 1854, that is, a few days after her wedding, Elisabeth wrote:

If only I had always stayed
on freedom's pathway blessed.
If only I had never strayed
in vanity. Distressed,

I wake up in a dungeon,
And chains are on my hands.
E'er stronger grows my longing.
Freedom flees to other lands!

Awakened from a frenzied dream
that held my spirit in its thrall,
I fled this error fruitlessly
in which I lost my freedom, all.

Left page: Empress Elisabeth, anonymous portrait, around 1855.
Above: Empress Elisabeth, portrait by Anton Einsle, 1856.

SCHÖNBRUNN
The imperial summer residence, Schönbrunn Palace

Schönbrunn Palace was originally built at the end of the 17th century by court architect Johann Bernhard Fischer von Erlach for Emperor Joseph I. In the mid 18th century it was expanded and completed by Nicola Pacassi, since from April until October Empress Maria Theresia made the originally private palace the official summer residence of the court and moved from the Hofburg to Schönbrunn with her entire court household. Franz Joseph and Elisabeth remained true to this tradition, with Sissi loving the vast palace park in which she went horse riding or walking every day.

Above: Schloss Schönbrunn, view from the parade court.

Below right: The bedroom of the Imperial couple in Schönbrunn Palace: Beds made of heavy rosewood.

FAMILY LIFE

The imperial couple's first daughter, who was named after the emperor's mother Sophie, was born on 5 March 1855. A year later, on 5 July 1856, their second daughter Gisela was born. However the harmonious family life was tarnished by the emergence of disputes between Elisabeth and her mother-in-law. The archduchess was used to everyone in the court being subordinate to her ideas, yet Elisabeth's growing popularity increased her self-confidence, and the young empress began to rebel against her powerful mother-in-law. The reason was the difference of ideas about the accommodation of the children. After her move to the new apartments in the Hofburg, Elisabeth also wanted to have her children with her. Sophie pleaded for the children's room to be kept near her own apartment. Yet it wasn't as if Archduchess Sophie wanted to "take" Elisabeth's children away from her out of cold-heartedness or malice. In her opinion, the place of an empress was at the side of her husband. Because of this she believed that Sissi didn't have the time to look after her children, which is why she found it more logical to have the children closer to her.

Elisabeth was able to get her own way, but in 1857 they experienced a great shock that would change everything. Against her mother-in-law's advice, Elisabeth took her children with her on a trip to Hungary, on which both girls fell ill. Yet, while the little Gisela recovered quickly, Sophie died at the age of two. Elisabeth was distraught. She blamed herself for the tragedy because she had insisted on taking the children with her, and from this time onwards, left Gisela entirely in the care of her mother-in-law.

Even after the long desired birth of the heir to the throne, Crown Prince Rudolf in August 1858, Sophie would remain the primary caretaker for the children. Elisabeth, however, began to suffer from poor health, suffered insomnia, lost her appetite and acquired a persistent cough. She refused to attend public appointments and appearances and thus not only caused displeasure at the Viennese court. Emperor Franz Joseph also showed little compassion for his wife, the consequences were arguments, disputes and jealousy. Elisabeth's reaction to the situation was to escape.

Left page: Crown Prince Rudolf with his sister Archduchess Gisela, around 1861.
Above: Elisabeth with her two children Gisela and Rudolf shortly after the birth of the crown prince in the year 1858.

This photo of the imperial family on the Schönbrunn Palace terrace is the only photo that shows Elisabeth with her family.

The Imperial couple's youngest daughter, Archduchess Marie Valerie, was born in 1868 and became known as the empress' favourite child and was allowed to spend the most time with her mother.

To her grandchildren Archduchess Sophie was a loving grandmother to whom they had an intimate relationship. That she took the children away from her daughter-in-law is not true to historical fact.

Elisabeth in her travel outfit. Coloured lithography by Eduard Kaiser, 1855.

Elisabeth in 1861 in Funchal, Madeira.

Empress Elisabeth surrounded by her court ladies on Madeira.

ESCAPE

In the first four years of her marriage, Elisabeth had given birth to three children; lost her eldest daughter; suffered a very difficult birth with the crown prince, from which she took a long time to recover. She felt abandoned by Franz Joseph and only wanted to get as far away as possible from the court. A very welcome reason for an extended absence was an illness. Whether Elisabeth was actually seriously ill and which illness she actually suffered from cannot be clearly discerned. The empress may have been coughing, but a serious lung or heart disease was, at least from a doctor's perspective, not diagnosed. However, the lung specialist Dr Skoda recommended a stay at a health resort. So the empress travelled to Madeira, where her cough and also the melancholy she had suffered in Vienna, improved. Elisabeth, who in Vienna had always felt alienated, for the first time became the centre of attention here and gained self-confidence. However, after seven months on Madeira Elisabeth became restless and decided to leave – not for Vienna, but embarked on an extended Mediterranean journey, which would take her all the way to Greece. Upon leaving Madeira she wrote: "Every ship I see leaving awakens the greatest desire in me to be on it – whether going to Brazil, Africa or the Cape is all the same. I just don't want to have to be stuck in one place ..." This actually defined her future life motto. When Elisabeth returned to the Viennese court after her two-year absence she had undergone a profound change. From the charming but shy girl had become a self-assured, proud beauty. Elisabeth had recognised the power of her beauty and from now on, used it for her own interests.

Empress Elisabeth, photograph by Ludwig Angerer taken in autumn 1860, shortly before the empress left for Madeira.

"SHE WORSHIPPED HER BEAUTY LIKE A HEATHEN HIS IDOLS"
The cult of beauty

Both the men and women of Elisabeth's time raved about her beauty – where it was actually the grace, radiance and secretive air that surrounded her they were more attracted to. As mentioned, the empress recognised the power of her beauty, thus her beauty care took up a large part of her daily routine. In order to maintain her much admired beauty she tried out countless beauty recipes, which were prepared for her each day at the court pharmacy. Her favourite cream was the so-called Crème Céleste, which consisted of soft wax, spermaceti, sweet almond oil and glycerine, and, due to her wishes – as with all her creams – had to be odourless because she rejected any type of perfume. Because the empress spent a lot of time outdoors and on her rides, mountain hikes and ocean cruises was subjected more often to the sun, she also had the so-called Wilson cream developed – the first sun cream with the mineral basis of zinc and talc, because tanned skin was seen as an absolute beauty flaw, the most important beauty ideal being white "porcelain complexion". At the same time, the whitish cream had the advantage of also making undesired

tanned skin appear whiter. The empress also loved facial masks made from pressed strawberries, which like the modern fruit acid creams had a tightening and refreshing effect. One particularly unusual "anti-ageing measure" was, however, a face leather mask, fitted with raw veal inside and which she wore over-night and had the effect of radical scavengers.

Elisabeth was particularly proud of her thick, knee-length hair, which was brushed two to three hours a day – long hair at the time being considered as one of the essential beauty features of a woman. Elisabeth used her daily hairdressing appointments, which had a somewhat cult-like procedure to them, to learn various different languages and to study the culture of ancient Greece. Her hairdresser Franziska "Fanny" Feifalik played an important role here. The former hairdresser of the Vienna Burgtheater was responsible for the artful hairstyles of the empress and, after the hours of hairdressing, braiding and pinning up the masses of hair, had to show in a silver bowl the hair that had fallen out. Every fourteen days her hair was washed with an especially created mixture of

Left page: Elisabeth in the bright morning light. Painting by Franz Xaver Winterhalter, 1864.
Above: The empress' dressing table in the Vienna Hofburg.

Empress Elisabeth, photo by Ludwig Angerer, 1863/64

"Light dress" of the empress. Elisabeth constantly made sure that her dresses emphasised her slim figure and her unbelievable waistline of 51 centimetres.

egg yolk and cognac and then rinsed with a concoction called lavender spirit, which increased the circulation,. The procedure took a whole day; in later years Elisabeth was suspected of having had her hair coloured with indigo and a nut extract.

Elisabeth's beauty cult developed into a lifetime task and finally took on proportions about which her niece Marie Larisch rather negatively said: "She worshipped her beauty like a heathen his idols, down on her knees. The sight of the perfection of her body gave her aesthetic pleasure; anything that tainted this perfection to her was inartistic and abhorrent." Because Elisabeth apparently drew her self-confidence exclusively from her beauty, she also panicked about ageing and, as she aged, hid her face behind umbrellas and fans – in her opinion, however, these were not only supposed to hide her disappearing beauty but also act as a symbolic barrier between herself and her surroundings.

Aside from her beauty regime the empress also dedicated a great part of her day to maintaining her slim figure, which admittedly didn't fit the beauty ideal of the

era at all – which preferred rounder, full-bodied women. Elisabeth was 172cm tall and weighed between 48 and 50 kilograms. Her waist measured 51cm, whereby one shouldn't forget that women of the time were laced and wore corsets from an early age. In order to stay slim she did sport every day – apart from her riding, other sports she enjoyed were fencing, swimming and hiking. To stay fit and flexible, Elisabeth also engaged in a daily gymnastics programme, which she did directly in her dressing room and which also received great attention. In his memoirs, her Greek reader, Constantine Christomanos, described his impressions of the exercising empress in the following way: "Today, before we left, she called me back into her salon. At the open door between the salon and her bedroom she had ropes, bars and rings installed. When I saw her she was just raising herself on the hand rings. She was wearing a black silk dress with a long train, hemmed with magnificent black ostrich feathers. I had never seen her so pompously dressed. Hanging on the ropes, she made a fantastic impression, a creature something between a snake and a bird."

Above: Elisabeth before a night sky. Painting by Franz Xaver Winterhalter, 1864. Elisabeth used her daily hairdressing sessions to learn languages; her reader Constantin Christomanos described the almost cult-like procedure of the hairdressing in his memoirs: "'It always takes about two hours,' she said, 'and while my hair is so busy my mind is idle. I am afraid it escapes from the hair on my head to the fingers of my hairdresser. That is why my head hurts so much' ... The empress sat at a table, pulled into the middle of the room and laid with a white table cloth, in a white peignoir, with open hair that reached the floor and which could enwrap her whole being."

Above: Dressing gown.
Below Left: The empress' travel toiletry kit.

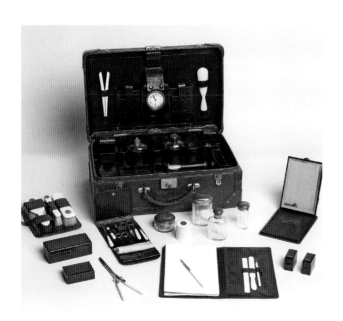

Even her style of dress was not in keeping with the fashion of the time, for Elisabeth placed great importance on her clothes emphasising her slim figure, and thus refrained from wearing crinolines and bulgy underskirts. At the same time, her clothes had to allow her a lot of freedom of movement and had to be comfortable. The most remarkable of these were her shoes. As "first lady" she didn't wear silk ankle boots with a heel, but comfortable, flat leather shoes − mostly ankle-high, lace-up boots in which she could carry out her extended walks and hikes − even in bad weather.

The legend that Elisabeth starved herself all her life in order to remain slim must be dispelled. Original menus show that Elisabeth did indeed have a healthy appetite. A normal breakfast consisted of coffee with cold or warm cream, sweet or savoury pastries, eggs, cold meats, honey, fruit and various biscuits and bread rolls. This was accompanied by a glass of wine. For lunch she usually had roasts with vegetables, and in the afternoon, afternoon tea. Receipts from various bakeries show that Elisabeth liked to eat desserts and mainly sorbet.

ERZSÉBET KIRÁLYNÉ
QUEEN ELISABETH OF HUNGARY

Elisabeth had little interest in active politics and only got involved once in the governing rule of her husband – to speak up for Hungary. Elisabeth felt a great attachment to the spirited and proud Hungarian folk, which since the bloody repression of the revolution by Franz Joseph in the year 1849 had been ruled with absolutism. On Madeira, her favourite court lady, Caroline "Lilly" Hunyady, had told the empress about her Hungarian homeland and had awakened Elisabeth's interest. From 1863 she learned Hungarian and took a young girl, which went against the tradition of court not being of aristocratic lineage, as a reader to the Viennese court: Ida Ferenczy, who would become her closest confidante and best friend. And because Ida was acquainted with the Hungarian liberals Gyula Andrássy and Franz Deák, she used her position to introduce the empress. Elisabeth became a glowing advocate of Hungarian interests and a huge hope of the leading representative of the Hungarians, who for the first time since Maria Theresia put their trust in a member of the imperial family. Without a doubt, she played a large role in Franz Joseph's signing the reconciliation in 1867 after long negotiations, which recognised the historical rights of Hungary and founded the Austro-Hungarian dual monarchy. In the same year, in St. Mathew's church in Budapest, the ceremonious coronation took place in which also Elisabeth was crowned the Queen of Hungary.

Oh Hungary beloved land,
I see you now in chains.
If only I could rescue you,
But slavery remains!

"If I Could Grant You All a King!", 1886

Left page: Elisabeth as Queen of Hungary, historical photography by Emil Rabending, 1866. The photo series of the empress was already taken a few months before the official coronation in 1867.
Above: As a symbol of appreciation for the empress' vehement campaigning for Hungary she was crowned Queen of Hungary together with Franz Joseph.

Elisabeth as Hungarian queen, Viktor Tilgner, 1879. "For her part, the empress loved the Hungarians, their knightly character, their love for riding, horses, fiery dances, yearning gypsy ways … so very much coincided with her own feelings and being, above all else." (Eugen Ketterl, valet to Emperor Franz Joseph)

Rumours of a supposed relationship of the empress with the leader of the Hungarian liberals and later prime minister, Gyula Graf Andrássy, have to be relegated to the realm of legend.

Below: Celebrated by Hungary's dignitaries: The coronation of the Imperial couple on 8 June 1867 in St. Mathew's church.

GÖDÖLLÖ
Elisabeth's private refuge in Hungary

On the occasion of their coronation, the Imperial couple was presented with Gödöllö Castle by the Hungarian Nation, which was also a sign of gratitude for Elisabeth's support during the negotiations for the Austro-Hungarian Compromise. The baroque summer castle was originally built in the mid 18th century for Antal Graf Grassalkovich, and was remodelled and extended by Elisabeth according to her very personal taste. The rooms were thus decorated in violet colours, and a large riding arena and a circus ring made it possible for her to follow her favourite past time, riding, undisturbed. Elisabeth also insisted on Gödöllö being seen as a private refuge and because of this, the court etiquette otherwise observed was not practiced there. She also managed to have people invited to Gödöllö who were not 'able of court' and were never allowed to enter the Hofburg or Schönbrunn Palace. For this reason, Elisabeth spent a lot of time in Gödöllö, where she felt free and unconstrained, was able to exclusively follow her own interests and to surround herself with people whom she liked and who shared her great love of riding.

"NEVER A MORE AUDACIOUS AND AT THE SAME TIME TRULY MORE LOVELY PARFORCE RIDER"
Riding as a high-performance sport

Since her childhood, riding had always been one of Elisabeth's greatest passions, which she also inherited from her father, Duke Max. Now, as empress, she began to train hard and aspired to be one of the best and courageous female riders in Europe. First she participated in the hunts in Gödöllö in Hungary, but the terrain soon proved too little an athletic challenge for her. Demanding and wild hunts were a great joy to her; this took her to England, where the famous parforce hunts took place – extended pack hunting across free terrain with the jumping of obstacles such as hedges, walls and ditches. As her pilot, who functioned as her riding guide and instructor, she was given one of the best riders in England, Scotsman Officer William George "Bay" Middleton. Middleton, who at first was not very happy to have to look after an empress, was impressed by the empress' courage and stamina. With his help, at the hunting races of sometimes up to one-hundred riders or in which only a handful made it to the finish, Elisabeth was the only woman to complete the race. A hunt reporter of Baily's Magazine raved that there had never been "a more audacious and at the same time truly more lovely parforce rider". Elisabeth loved the athletic challenge; was admired by her chaper-

ones for her courage, skill and stamina, and was proud to be the only woman – that is, in a woman's saddle – to finish and the only one who also never had a bad fall.

At the end of the 1870s Elisabeth heard that the most technically challenging hunts were held in Ireland. The small enclosures, larger, compact embankments and broad, open ditches were a welcome challenge to prove her ability. During her riding sojourns Elisabeth was also in a glowing mood – never melancholy, sick or moody. At these riding events she was always described as being cheerful and charming; she never withdrew, and loved the regular high-spirited evening dinner parties. In Vienna she hated such similar functions.

Elisabeth may have detested her obligations as empress, but she made the most of the positive accompanying perks as a matter of course. The riding trips and sojourns were taken with a large entourage of personnel, from grooms and royal household to the empress' riding friends, for which a fitting castle was always rented. The stays and trips cost a fortune – her journey to Ireland alone cost over 158,000 guilders – which is about 1.4 million euros. Franz Joseph paid every time without objection – out of his own pocket.

Left page: Empress Elisabeth on a horse in front of Possenhofen Palace. Painting by Carl Piloty.
Above: The empress always had a heavy leather fan with her, which she could quickly open when curious observers came near, in order to protect herself from their enquiring stares.

POETIC DREAM WORLDS

From a very early age, Elisabeth wrote mostly longing and rapturous poems. She loved poetry, revered the Greek poets, mainly Homer, and was a great lover of Shakespeare. *A Midsummer Night's Dream* was one of her favourite pieces, and in her many of her poems she also compared herself to the fairy queen Titania. From the 1880s, the empress virtually escaped to the world of poetry and felt increasingly unsettled by everything else. Her biggest idol and role model became Heinrich Heine, whom she called her "master" in her poems:

I hurry to the land of dreams,
My master, it is you.
My soul rejoices with delight
And sings your praises, too!

Elisabeth's worship of the poet, who died in 1856, could also be seen as a symbol of her autonomy and independence. At that time, Heine was by far not the recognised "prince among poets" that he is considered today, but it was exactly his realistic contemporary criticism and irony, which was so scandalous for many, that attracted her. Sissi's own poems were mostly characterised by wistfulness and melancholy, and expressed how misunderstood and lonely and unhappy she felt. She wrote of her disappointment, her sadness and her longings, and in later poems she also expressed her increasing contempt for mankind and her isolation.

But her poems also frequently contained irony and also sarcasm. Her Habsburg relatives, to whom she had a divided relationship, she attacked again and again. Many members of the Viennese court were afraid of her sharp tongue and her pen – justifiably so. For in these poems she openly denounced the hypocrisy, the fakeness and the haughtiness of court society and openly also settled open scores with the imperial family:

Original lapis lazuli writing set of the empress.

The temple with the statue of Elisabeth's deeply respected poet, Heinrich Heine, in the Achilleion park.

They're not unlike a fat Swiss cow:
So broad and corpulent.
And yet they think themselves endowed
With beauty that God sent.

Themselves as ugly as a witch
Found in a fairy tale,
They pull to pieces everyone,
Disparage without fail.

Attired in glaring peacock garb
And risible toupees.
Mocking laughter can't conceal
The error of their ways.

Family Meal, 1887

However, the criticism of the Viennese court was not the most important subject of the empress' verse:

Out in the world Titania shall not go,
A world where she is never understood,
Where countless crowds of gapers seek to know
More of her "foolish sense" of womanhood.
Malevolence and envy are on show
And misinterpret every act of good.
She longs to live in regions that are known
For harbouring souls in keeping with her own.

To Titania, 1888

I wander in my solitude on earth below.
My back is turned on pleasure and on life.
I have no one to share the longings of my soul,
No one to understand and ease my strife.

I flee before the world and all its pleasure;
and its inhabitants seem far from me.
Their joy, their grief are things I cannot measure.
I wander in my solitude: I'm free.

The things that caused me pain I've learned to cherish.
My solitude is now a paradise.
My spirit can unfold its wings in freedom;
My isolation is a fitting price.

To Future Souls, Ischl, June 1887 (Winterlieder)

Mankind I would abandon
along with life's own pain,
and all my daily efforts,
all that I loathe in vain.

Whither?, July 1887 (Winterlieder)

Though I wander with the others,
I am not the same as they.
Viewing me with deep suspicion,
their displeasure they betray.

Though I Wander, 1888 (Third Book)

Original poetry book of Empress Elisabeth. According to the wishes of the empress, the original is still in the Swiss national archive in Bern today.

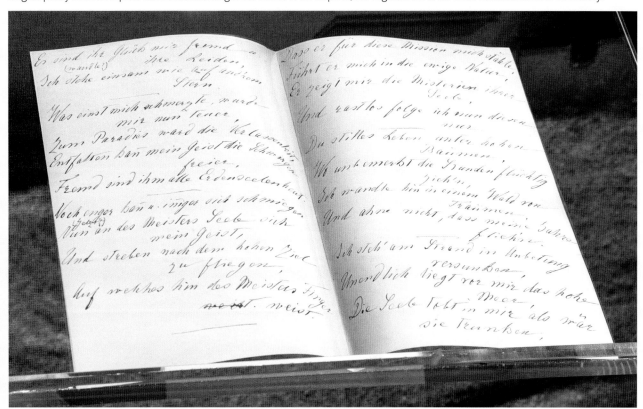

CASTLE OF DREAMS
Hermesvilla

The construction of Villa Waldruh, as it was formerly called, in the Lainzer Tiergarten in Vienna was begun in 1881 according to designs by Ringstrasse architect Carl Hasenauer, who at the time was also entrusted with the building of the Hofburg theatre and the court museums as well as later, the new Hofburg. Franz Joseph had the villa consigned to Elisabeth as private ownership, which saw it defined as a clear private refuge of the empress. Franz Joseph had probably hoped to bind Elisabeth more closely to Vienna and thus also to spend more time with her. The Hermesvilla was furnished and furbished exactly according to her desires. Because she was such a huge admirer of Shakespeare and loved *A Midsummer Night's Dream* and in many of her poems compared herself to Shakespeare's fairy queen Titania, Franz Josef he had her bedroom in the Hermesvilla painted with scenes from the play. Unfortunately he didn't quite manage to capture her taste, and Franz Joseph remarked resigned, "I will always be afraid of ruining everything". However, as often as it was said that Elisabeth hated the Hermesvilla, it wasn't true. She loved the isolation of the Lainzer Tiergarten, the original nature and the many animals in the park, and regularly spent several weeks to months here in spring. Most often in May, she came directly to the Hermesvilla after her travels; met her daughters and Franz Joseph, who loved these weeks with his family, and stayed, apart from a few breaks, usually until the end of June. In 1888 she raved about in one of her poets about the "castle of her dreams".

Titania wanders under tow'ring trees;
White petals have been strewn across her way.
The beeches and the old oaks are in leaf,
a vast cathedral in the month of May.

A fairy-story dream fills the cathedral,
A place of magic, unseen and concealed,
Where coral bells are ringing their sweet music,
And butterflies in splendour are revealed.

Left, above: Hermes statue in front of Villa Hermes in the Lainzer Tiergarten
Left, below: Detail of the wall painting in the empress' exercise room, in the "style of Pompeii", which depicts various types of sport.
Right page, above: The Hermesvilla was a present from Emperor Franz Joseph to his wife and was meant to serve as a refuge in Vienna.
Right page, below: The empress' bedroom was decorated with frescoes, which depict scenes from her favourite work, *A Midsummer Night's Dream,* by William Shakespeare.

"WITH A SIGH, AT LAST I'M FREE TO TAKE THE CROWN FROM MY TIRED HEAD"
Representation, court balls, silver wedding anniversary

From the very beginning, Elisabeth found her ceremonial duties bothersome and unpleasant and had felt that at representative appearances she was paraded like a horse "in harness". After having learned over time how to stand up for herself at the Viennese court, and when she finally refused to play the role of empress, she was in Vienna less often. The empress spent a fortune on her expensive entertainment such as riding and travelling and hardly took part in appearances of the imperial house at all anymore. With her eccentric lifestyle and demonstrative disinterest she increasingly annoyed the public. For example, the opening of the Vienna opera house was especially rescheduled for her because she stayed in Hungary longer than expected. She still didn't attend the opening because she didn't feel well.

Elisabeth took less and less care not to disappoint people and designed her life only according to her priorities. Although there were recurring allusions to the seldom presence of the empress Franz Joseph stood firmly at his wife's side, and Elisabeth herself was not the least bit interested in public opinion. The silver wedding of the imperial couple in the year 1879 would finally be the last public appearance of the empress. Franz Joseph

implored his wife to this time stand by him – for his sake she allowed herself to be "harnessed". The event was held with great pomp, and the appearance of the empress at the celebrations caused a sensation. Elisabeth seemed to be glowing, beautiful, gracious and charming. She completed the entire programme with the emperor – including the receptions and homages of the representatives of the crown lands, diplomats and European regents, which lasted more than three days.

From the age of thirty Elisabeth had not allowed herself to be photographed, and then, from the age of forty, no longer allowed herself to be painted, so quite early on reporters were given photo montages. In addition, as she soon would retire from public life, the newspapers were given fantasy depictions – in order to uphold the illusion of the empress as sovereign to the public, at least for a while. The templates used were the last original pictures that Elisabeth had had made at the end of the 1860s aged thirty, which now had been manipulated with creative retouching depending on the occasion, and were put together for family or representation collages. In this way, Elisabeth was allowed to age in an artificially cultivated way, and altered her hairstyle according to the current trends.

Left page: Portrait of Elisabeth in ruby jewellery, painted on the occasion of her silver wedding in 1879 by Georg Raab, is the last authentic portrait of the empress – twenty years before her death.
Above: Court ball in 1886 in the Zeremoniensaal of the Hofburg, after a drawing by Wilhelm Gause.

"A SEAGULL, I AM NOT FROM ANY LAND"
Restlesss roaming

His whole life, Franz Joseph loved his wife above everything and fulfilled her every wish. Only with his support – also financially – was she able to lead and finance her independent life and her extravagant trips and her refuges. Franz Joseph considered himself first an emperor and then a husband. Fulfilling his obligations had top priority; the personal always came second. Elisabeth felt exactly the opposite. But because Franz Josef loved her above all else, he made it possible for her to realise an autonomous and independent life – even if that meant that he had to live without her, because Elisabeth didn't feel up to being at his side. After the empress had finally freed herself from her duties as empress and was only seldom in Vienna, a friendly marriage developed – albeit due to the distance – in which both of them always appreciated and respected each other. When Elisabeth was travelling the two wrote to each other almost daily. These were not, as is sometimes maintained, superficial letters of duty, but comprehensive, funny representations of their individual experiences, impressions and news. In all his letters the emperor expressed his great longing

for her and she always began with, "My dearest Sissi Angel", or "Beloved Sissi", and ended with "Your most loving Mannikin".

Furthermore, the imperial couple saw each other more often than was portrayed. Up until her death they met every year regularly for a few days at the Hermesvilla in Vienna, mostly together with their daughters, and for a few days in Hungary and in summer in Ischl. The nicest time they spent together was each early summer, when they met privately for a few days on the Cote d'Azur. Elisabeth looked forward to these meetings and always arrived much earlier in order to prepare everything for Franz Joseph. She found new walking paths and organised excursions and pleasant evenings, which as an exception they spent all alone. After these harmonious days they went their separate ways.

Even years later, these partings affected Franz Joseph. In the year 1897, after one of these short meetings, he wrote, "Édes szeretett lelkem (my sweet, beloved soul), After such endlessly short togetherness we are yet again limited to the written word. This is very sad, but there is

Left page: Franz Joseph and Elisabeth in the hotel garden in Cape Martin, after a painting by Wilhelm Gause.
Above: In order to have his "angel Sissi" with him also when she was on long trips, in the offices of all his residences in which he spent a great part of the day the emperor surrounded himself with many portraits and photos of his wife. Directly in front of his desk in the Hofburg on an easel was his favourite portrait – Elisabeth with her hair open by Franz Xaver Winterhalter.

nothing to be done about it. Our recent parting affects me a great deal ... "

As she grew older, the empress became more and more restless and unsettled, and her travelling, which she had originally been able to justify for health reasons, became her life's main occupation. She wanted to visit new countries and get to know new cultures. But not only that. Mainly, she enjoyed the carefree life without duties or limitations; to do what she loved to do. She refused to play the role of the empress of Austria, but took advantage of all the associated amenities, above all financial, as a matter of course.

The diary of her favourite servant, Leopold Alram, tells of carefree days on the Cote d'Azur, which were characterised mainly by visits to pastry shops; shopping and visits on the yachts of rich Americans or European moneyed aristocracy such as the Rothschilds. Elisabeth loved not only the sophisticated but occasionally also enjoyed the very simple. While out on her hikes, she liked to patronise simple alpine huts or village pubs for a glass of milk or some pretzels along with a glass of beer. The main thing was to remain unrecognised; as soon as she had the feeling that she was being observed, she fled immediately.

However Elisabeth did not travel throughout the world aimlessly. On the contrary. A year in advance, she would plan her travel routes exactly; only her closest trusted servants and attendants were told and bound to a strict silence. Franz Joseph fulfilled his beloved wife's every desire, as before. Only with his support – also financially – was she able to embark on and finance her independent life and extended journeys. Elisabeth mostly loved ship cruises; felt magically drawn to the vast ocean and dreamed about flying free like a seagull in it in her poems:

A seagull, I am not from any land;
My home cannot be found on any strand;
Unbound by any situation,
I make any wave my station.

North Sea Songs 7, 1885

In the empress' first-aid kit, which she carried with her, there was also a cocaine serum, cocaine being a completely harmless medicament for depressions and state of exhaustion, which one could get over the counter at pharmacies.

DESTINATIONS AND MODES OF TRANSPORT
Imperial saloon car, ships ...

For most of her journeys the empress used an especially built imperial saloon car, which consisted of a saloon and a sleeping car; had electric lighting, steam heating and a toilet for the empress. Of course, her personnel travelled more modestly. The accompanying chambermaid slept on a sofa, which took up the whole breadth of its tiny space that was separated from the sleeping area of the empress. In addition, Elisabeth travelled with her personal furniture and horses, which were transported in their own carriages. The court trains had a separate schedule, priority above all other trains, and during night trips the speed was restricted in order to allow comfortable sleep.

The empress undertook most of her ocean trips on the imperial yacht, which was simple but elegant and magnificently furnished. The rooms reserved for the empress in the hull of the ship may have looked like a sailor's quarters and were simply and practically outfitted – all furniture was covered with white linen sheets – but it was important for the empress to decorate with large flower arrangements. But she didn't want to go without certain amenities. These included a daily bath, which she usually took in the early morning. While on ocean trips, she only wanted to bathe in sea water, barrels of sea water were hauled aboard and her bath filled with it. So that the water didn't get spilled during her baths, the ship had to anchor while she was bathing. Apart from this, she didn't give up her daily ritual of daily drinking fresh milk, for which goats from her dairy were especially taken along.

On the deck of the yacht there was a glass pavilion, which offered a 360 degree view of the ocean. Elisabeth didn't suffer from sea sickness and loved the high seas because she felt particularly close to the elements. She explained to Christomanos: "When it is stormy and we are on the high seas I usually let myself be tied to this chair. I do this like Odysseus because I feel drawn (in) by the waves."

The original court salon carriage in which Elisabeth travelled can be viewed in the Technical Museum Vienna.

ACHILLEION "ASYLUM"

Over the years, Elisabeth developed a great affection for Greece, loved the history, culture and landscape of the country. Her first sojourn there was on Corfu in the year 1861 – on the way back from Madeira to Vienna. She could not discard her longing for the Greek island and, so, in 1888 she decided to build her refuge here, which she named after Achilles, her favourite hero in Greek mythology. The magnificent villa was built by Neapolitan architect Raffaele Carito in the style of Pompeii and was furnished with valuable antiques. Elisabeth was enthusiastic about the thought of being able to design a home entirely according to her ideas, and named the Achilleion "... my asylum, where I can belong to myself alone..." This is where Elisabeth wanted to make her last home, and her family was happy that it seemed that she had finally found her port, her sanctuary. However within a short period, the restless empress lost interest in her Achilleion and felt burdened and constricted by it.

Elisabeth now only wanted to travel, and decided, to the great chagrin of the emperor, who had just spent a fortune on it, to sell the Achilleion.

Above: The statue of the dying Achilles by Ernst Herter in the Achilleion garden, named after the empress' favourite hero from the Greek antiquities.

Below left: A park of legends: entrance to Achilleion

Below right: The empress' jewellery box from Achilleion

Above und below: The peristyle of Achilleion, the Mediterranean refuge of the empress.

"MATER DOLOROSA"
Strokes of fate

Creating a turning point in the empress' life was the suicide of her only son, Crown Prince Rudolf, in 1889. Born in 1858, the heir to the crown had been very similar to his mother as a child and, at her instigation, received a liberal education, which made him an open-minded, interested man who detested the aristocratic way of life. His private circles consisted mainly of liberal intellectuals and scientists, for which he was harshly criticised by the conservative and clerically characterised Viennese court and because of which he made enemies in politically intellectual circles. Rudolf's political views became increasingly opposing to the official politics of the court and forced him into a life full of secrets. For years, Rudolf fought for a duty that was consistent with his abilities, but at that time of his life was ignored by his father.

From 1888, Rudolf's mood drastically changed. His failed struggle for recognition from his father, his failed marriage with Stephanie of Belgium and numerous affairs had made the 30-year-old Rudolf a desperate and resigned person. However, Empress Elisabeth was of no help to her son during this difficult time. She was too involved in her own life to recognise Rudolf's cynicism behind his increasing despair. On 30 January 1889, Rudolf shot himself along with this lover, the 17-year-old Baroness Mary Vetsera, who was prepared to die with him, in the hunting lodge Mayerling. The tragic suicide of her only son Rudolf was for Elisabeth not only a huge shock, but also a turning point in her life. If the empress had already been becoming more and more melancholy, restless and unsettled, now she became bitter, and increasingly withdrew; she only wore black and became unsociable and unapproachable. The tragedy made it possible for her to finally retire from the public and stylise herself as a "mater dolorosa".

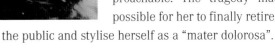

Left page: Empress Elisabeth. Posthumous portrait by Leopold Horowitz.
Above: That Rudolf was murdered can be excluded based alone on the presence of the dated farewell letters. The photo of the crown prince laid out also proves the fatal head injury from a gunshot.

Above: Rudolf with his wife Stephanie of Belgium in Laxenburg, the spring residency of the Habsburgs, south of Vienna.
Below, left: Heirs to the throne: Crown Prince Rudolf and Stephanie at their wedding in the year 1881.

Right page, above left: The seventeen-year-old baroness Mary Vetsera was the crown prince's last lover. However the murder and suicide was not a love story. Rudolf didn't want to die alone and in Mary, who was enraptured and in love, he found someone who was prepared to die with him.

Right page, above right: Crown Prince Rudolf shortly before his suicide in January 1889.

Right page, below: The hunting lodge Mayerling, location of the tragedy. In the early morning hours of 30 January 1889 Rudolf first shot Mary Vetsera and then himself. Because it was to be kept secret that a young girl died with the crown prince, Mary's family had to secretly transport the body of their daughter away from Mayerling under inhumane circumstances.

THE ASSASSINATION

I wanted my soul to fly away to heaven through a very small opening of my heart
Elisabeth to Baroness Rothschild the day before her death

In summer 1898, Elisabeth was stationed in Territet near Montreux for a few weeks and took numerous trips from there. On 9 September, Elisabeth and her court lady Irma Sztáray went to Prégny, to visit Baroness Rothschild. On the same day, Elsiabeth returned to Geneva and, as always, alighted under her less well-known title of Countess of Hohenembs at the Hotel Beau Rivage. An indiscretion led to, next day, a Geneva newspaper's publishing that the empress of Austria was staying in the hotel. This is how the Italian anarchist Luigi Lucheni, who had actually come to Geneva to assassinate the prince of Orléans, found out about the empress' stay. That the prince changed his travel route at the last minute and left Geneva earlier than planned didn't bother Lucheni much – by accident he had found a much more prominent victim. On 10 September, the empress left the hotel at lunchtime to go to the shipping pier where her ship to Montreux had been docked. On the way, Lucheni attacked the empress and thrust a sharpened triangular file into her breast. Elisabeth fell to the ground, but got up immediately and acted as if nothing had happened, thanks to the passersby who had helped her. No-one, not even Elisabeth herself – noticed the fatal injury. Lucheni had stabbed the empress right in the heart and her heart chamber was slowly filling with blood. Elisabeth went on board with her servant, but they had hardly embarked when the empress collapsed. When Irma Sztáray opened the empress' dress she discovered a small stain on her chamise, then the tiny stab wound that wasn't bleeding. Now she finally realised that Elisabeth had been fatally wounded. The ship turned around immediately and the dying empress was taken back to her hotel room, where doctors could only pronounce her dead at 2:40pm.

Her daughter Marie Valerie wrote in her journal: "Now it has happened just as she always wished: quickly, painlessly without medical consultations; without long, anxious days of worry for her loved ones." And when Franz Joseph received the news of her death from his aide-de-camp, Count Paar, his only words were: "You have no idea what this woman meant to me."

Left page: On 10 September 1898, on her way to the ship in Geneva Elisabeth was stabbed by the Italian anarchist Luigi Lucheni with a file Illustration in the magazine *Le Petit Journal* from 25 September 1898.
Above: Emperor Franz Joseph at the death bed of his wife. Lithography based on a photograph by Ludwig Angerer, 1898.

THE LEGEND OF SISI AND SISSI
The origins of an icon

Because Elisabeth withdrew early on from her public role as empress and avoided representative appearances, during her lifetime she was not the centre of public interest and was also not the all-round beloved, celebrated and beautiful empress who filled the front pages. Emperor Franz Joseph had a much more important role here. The "good old emperor" was anchored in the heart of the people – he got the sympathies. The situation however changed quickly when, after Elisabeth's murder, the economic potential of the beautifully, secretive and above all tragically murdered empress was recognised. This is how Elisabeth posthumously became the venerated, selfless and popular empress. A critical examination of her ambivalent personality, her egocentricity and egomania was completely excluded – and thus a false image was perpetrated. With enormous success, the "Sissi" trilogy by Ernst Marischka in the 1950s made Elisabeth the world-famous and celebrated "Sissi". Contributing to this was the enchanting interpretation of the historical figure by Romy Schneider, which today characterises the image of the young, warm, easy-going Sissi, but has very little in common with the real personality of Empress Elisabeth.

Left page: Conquered viewers' hearts by storm: Romy Schneider as "Sissi" in Ernst Marischka's film of the same name, 1955.
Above: The Sissi Museum in the Vienna Hofburg.

Photo credits

Willfried Gredler-Oxenbauer: 2/3, 5, 15 (above), 20 (below), 21, 22, 23, 26/27, 45, 46, 47, 52, 53, 63; IMAGNO/ Austrian Archives: Cover photos, 1, 4, 6, 9, 10, 11, 19 (above left), 20 (above), 25, 30 (above, below left), 31, 32 (above right), 34, 37 (above left), 43, 44 (right), 57, 59 (above left & below); IMAGNO/Gerhard Trumler: 18 (above), 24; IMAGNO/Wien Museum: 58 (above); IMAGNO/Österr. Volkshochschularchiv: 40 (below), 51, 55 (below); IMAGNO/ Schloß Schönbrunn Kultur- und Betriebsges. M. b. H.: 13 (Sissi Museum), 17, 27 (below, photo: Edgar Knaack), 35 (photo: Tina Dietz), 37 (below), 54 (below right, photo: Margherita Spiluttini); IMAGNO/ÖNB: 8 (below), 14, 15 (below), 16, 19 (above right & below), 29, 32 (above left), 33, 36 (above left), 38, 39, 40 (above left), 43, 50, 58 (below), 61; akg-images/picturedesk.com: 8 (above left); Sammlung Rauch/Interfoto/picturedesk.com: 8 (above right); Thomas Höfler/Interfoto/picturedesk.com: 60; Jean-François Deroubaix/ Eyedea/picturedesk.com: 48; Friedrich/Interfoto/picturedesk.com: 62; Kunsthistorisches Museum Wien: 12 (below); Wien Museum: 49; Österreichisches Staatsarchiv, Haus-, Hof- und Staatsarchiv: 18 (below), 28, 30 (below right), 59 (above right); Monika Levay: 36 (right), 37 (right); Rebasso, Wien: 7; © Bundesmobilienverwaltung; Collection: Bundesmobilienverwaltung; Location: Hofmobiliendepot, Furniture Museum Vienna; photo: Sanjiro Minamikawa: 44 (left); Wikimedia Commons: 12 (above), 30 (above right, photo: Josef Székely), 41 (photo: Andres Rus), 54 (above & left below, photo: Piotrus), 55 (above, photo: Piotrus), 56

The author

Katrin Unterreiner studied Art History and History at the University of Vienna. Until 2007 she was scientific director of the Imperial Apartments at the Vienna Hofburg and curator of the Sissi Museum. She made a name for herself with numerous exhibitions and publications on the subject of the Habsburgs and on the day-to-day culture of the Viennese court.

ISBN 978-3-85431-617-6

sty̲ria

© 2012 by Pichler Verlag
in the Styria GmbH & Co KG publishing group
Vienna · Graz · Klagenfurt

Books from the Styria publishing group can be purchased
at all book shops and also from the online shop.

styriabooks.at

Editor: Johannes Sachslehner
Translation: Mỹ Huê McGowran; Translation of poems: John Winbigler
Cover design: Bruno Wegscheider; Book design: Maria Schuster
Cover photos: IMAGNO/Austrian Archives
Reproduction: Pixelstorm, Vienna
7 6 5 4 3 2 1
Printing and binding: Druckerei Theiss GmbH, St. Stefan im Lavanttal
Printed in Austria